On the City Streets

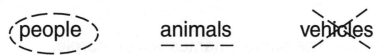

(people)   animals   ~~vehicles~~

Color the stores.

Do you see any plants? _____

Color Puzzle

The number names will be purple.

The color names will be red.

The boy's names will be black.

The girl's names will be yellow.

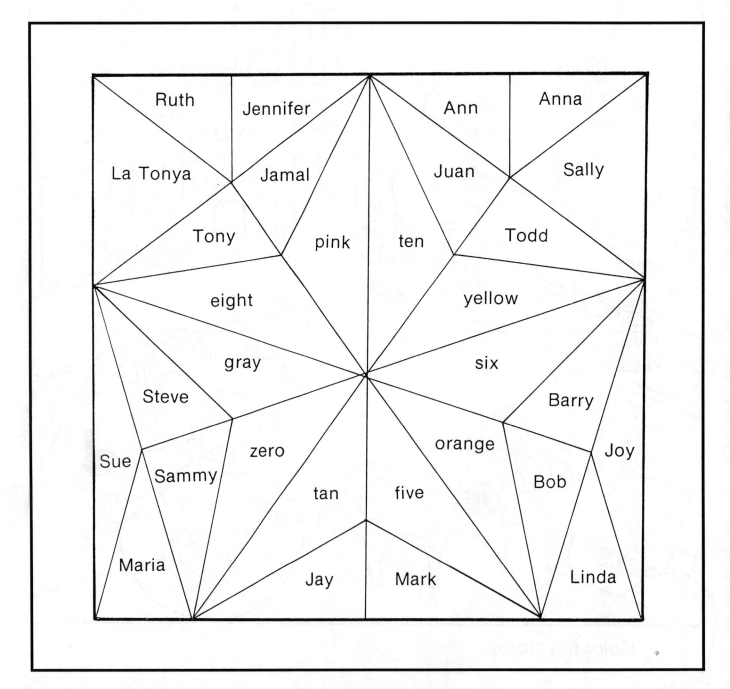

Ruth | Jennifer | Ann | Anna

La Tonya | Jamal | Juan | Sally

Tony | pink | ten | Todd

eight | yellow

gray | six

Steve | Barry

Sue | zero | orange | Joy

Sammy | tan | five | Bob

Maria | Jay | Mark | Linda

What Will You Find?

on a sandwich:

peanut butter
tuna fish
jam
cheese
butter
jellyfish
pickle
ham
hippo toes

in a closet:

jacket
hanger
dress
chicken leg
jeans
shirt
dinosaur track
shoe
beanstalk

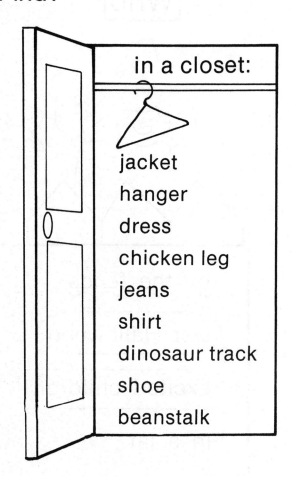

under my feet:

sand
the Earth
tree top
mud puddle
hawk
grass
rug
snail trail
dirt

over my head:

sun
rainbow
green grass
stars
hat
moon
sidewalk
footprints
cloud

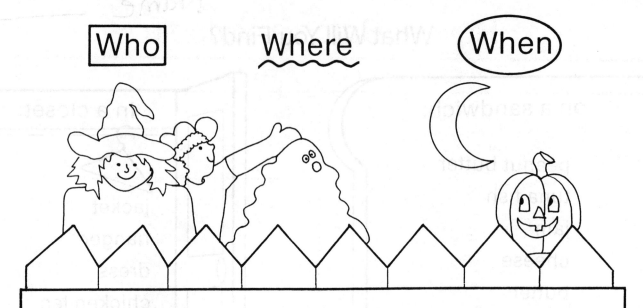

Who	Where	When

by the fence	during the night
last Halloween	under the table
excited children	a tired farmer
in a jar	in the lunch box
the funny clown	Ralph's grandfather
every day	after school
huge football players	tomorrow morning
around the school	the busy doctor
on my head	on my vacation

How many who words? _____

How many where words? _____

How many when words? _____

How to Catch a Tadpole

1. Read 2. Cut 3. Paste in order	
	1
	2
	3
	4
	5
	6

Put holes in the lid.

Look in the water until you see tadpoles.

Put the lid on the jar and take them home.

Find a jar at your house.

Go to a pond.

Scoop up some tadpoles in your jar.

The little tadpoles will grow up to be frogs.

Draw a big frog sitting on a log.
Make the log in a pond.

Write the Missing Letter

___ an

n ___ t

he ___

s ___ n

ba ___

___ id

be ___

___ op

w ___ g

___ up

si ___

j ___ t

Read and Answer

yes   no

1. Did the pig get in the mud? _____

2. Is the rat on the mat?

3. Is the pig wet?

4. Did the rat get a rag?

5. Is the bug big?

6. Is a hat on the pig?

Read and Answer

yes   no

1. Did the snake hide in the cave?

2. Did Kate ride up the hill?

3. Did Kate and Pete meet at the top?

4. Is it a hot day?

5. Did Pete hike up the hill?

6. Can a snake ride a bike?

Read and Draw

Put a green coat and hat on Gene.

Make three bees by the hive.

Make skates on Jane's feet.

Put five bats in the cave.

Make nine trees on the steep hill.

Make the cake brown and the rose yellow.

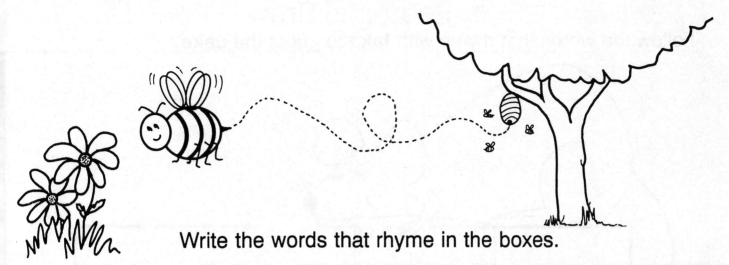

Write the words that rhyme in the boxes.

see	get	zoo

bow	bee	three
bet	shoe	set
we	too	wet
let	he	moo

Follow the words that rhyme with take to get to the cake.

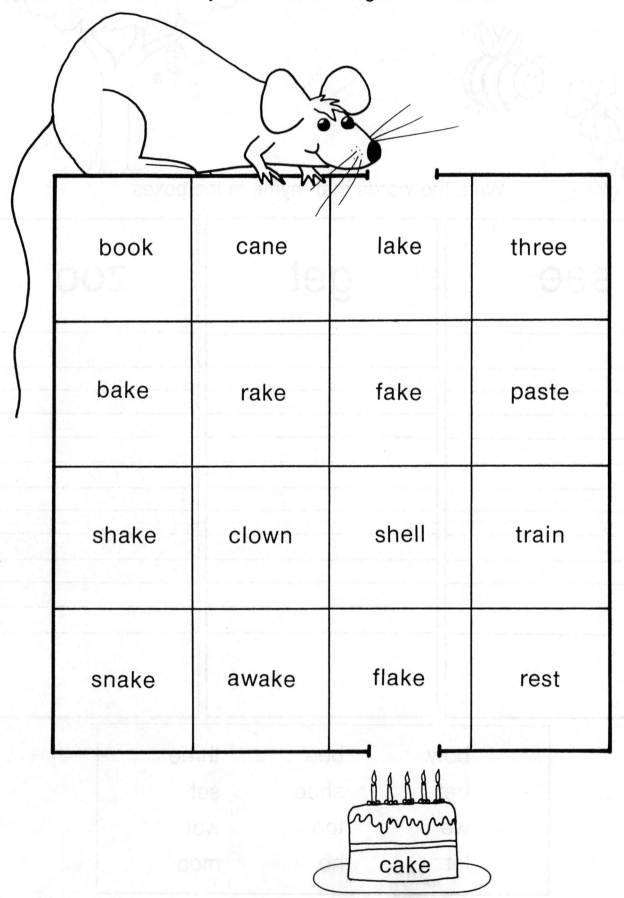

book	cane	lake	three
bake	rake	fake	paste
shake	clown	shell	train
snake	awake	flake	rest

cake

Fill in the blanks using rhyming words.

1. Put the _____ **wig** _____

on the _____ **pig** _____ .

2. He took his _____

to see the _____ .

3. A yellow _____

was on the _____ .

4. I put my _____

in the wet _____ .

5. She ate the _____

on that red _____ .

hand	pig
pet	fish
star	sand
wig	dish
vet	car

Making Big Words

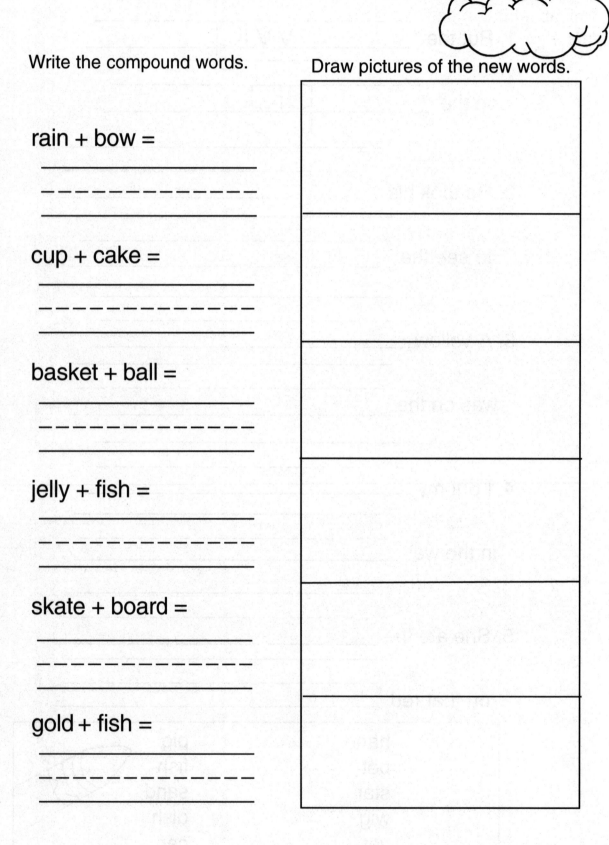

Write the compound words.

Draw pictures of the new words.

rain + bow =

_____

‒ ‒ ‒ ‒ ‒ ‒ ‒ ‒ ‒ ‒ ‒ ‒ ‒

_____

cup + cake =

_____

‒ ‒ ‒ ‒ ‒ ‒ ‒ ‒ ‒ ‒ ‒ ‒ ‒

_____

basket + ball =

_____

‒ ‒ ‒ ‒ ‒ ‒ ‒ ‒ ‒ ‒ ‒ ‒ ‒

_____

jelly + fish =

_____

‒ ‒ ‒ ‒ ‒ ‒ ‒ ‒ ‒ ‒ ‒ ‒ ‒

_____

skate + board =

_____

‒ ‒ ‒ ‒ ‒ ‒ ‒ ‒ ‒ ‒ ‒ ‒ ‒

_____

gold + fish =

_____

‒ ‒ ‒ ‒ ‒ ‒ ‒ ‒ ‒ ‒ ‒ ‒ ‒

Fill in the Blanks

Think about the underlined word.
Write a new word that means the same thing.

1. The <u>small</u> frog hopped into the pond. _____

2. I saw a <u>large</u> elephant at the zoo. _____

3. Did you hear the teacher <u>speak</u>? _____

4. Please <u>build</u> me a swing. _____

5. Don't <u>scream</u>, the baby is asleep. _____

6. Please <u>close</u> the door. _____

little	hard	big
make	leap	yell
shut	talk	fast

Name the Picture

Write two words that name each picture.

_____

_____

_____

_____

_____

_____

_____

_____

Word Box

baby	infant	scream
bright	jump	shiny
build	leap	sick
ill	make	yell

Match Opposites

Match.

tell	sour
hard	high
sweet	ask
low	soft
small	noisy
quiet	large
hot	first
last	cold

Homophones

Circle the right word.

1. Do you (know no) how to make your lunch?

2. I read a story about a brave (night knight).

3. Dad put a new (pane pain) of glass in the window.

4. Tim didn't (know no) the way to the store.

5. May I have a (peace piece) of pie?

6. How many (rose rows) of beans did you plant?

7. We had to wait an (our hour) to catch the bus.

8. Did you eat the (hole whole) pizza?

Read the Words

clown

gown

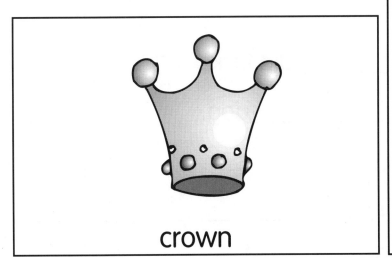

crown

down

brown

drown

gown

clown

frown

town

crown

I read these words to _____.

Write the name of the picture on the line.

crown

_____

_____

_____

Fill in the blanks.

1. She had a rip in her yellow _gown_.

2. The _cl_____ did tricks

   with a _br_____ dog.

3. The king went _d_____ _t_____

   to get his _cr_____.

I read these sentences to _____.

Read the story.
Put an X on the words that rhyme with <u>down</u>.

The Sad King

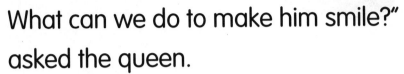

"The king is not happy.
See that big fro~~wn~~.
What can we do to make him smile?"
asked the queen.

"I saw a clown when I was downtown,"
said the prince.
We can get her to make the king smile."

The clown came in a funny, brown gown.
She did tricks for the king.

"I will not frown now," said the king.
"I like the tricks you did."
And the king gave the clown his crown.

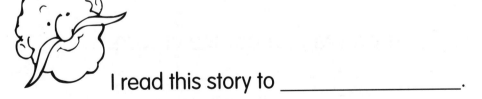

I read this story to _____.

Note: Your learner may need help reading the special words on this page.

| happy | smile | asked | prince | king | queen |

Telling Sentences

A **period** is used at the end of a sentence that tells you something.

Put a ꞏ at the end of the sentences.

1. I am Jim

2. My sister is Ann

3. We can go to the park

4. It will be fun

5. We will see lions

6. We will see monkeys

7. Then we can eat ice cream

Asking Sentences

A **question mark** is used at the end of a sentence that **asks** something.

Put a **?** at the end of the sentences.

1. Can you jump rope

2. Do you want to go to my house

3. Can we go to the pet shop

4. Was the dog funny

5. Is that a fox

6. What is that

7. Do you like pizza

Start at 1.
Connect the dots.

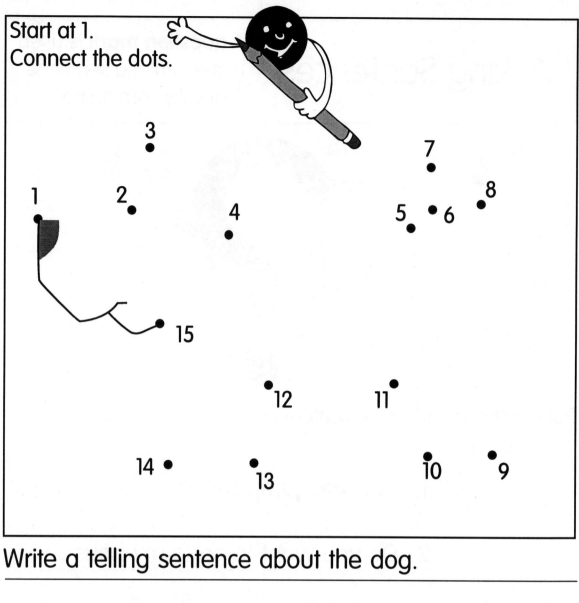

Write a telling sentence about the dog.

_____

- -

_____

- -

_____

Write an asking sentence about the dog.

_____

- -

_____

_____

- -

_____

Names start with capital letters.

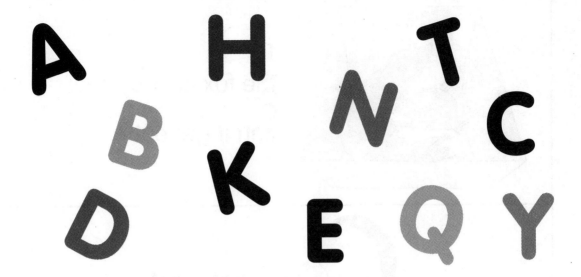

A B C D E F G H I J K L M N O P Q R S T U V W X Y Z

ann   A̲n̲n̲

bob   _____

kim   _____

dan   _____

jamal _____

ben   _____

jose   _____

nancy _____

My name is _____

Write capital letters.
Use periods or question marks.

T
~~the~~ fox is in a box.
C
~~can~~ it get out ?

is that a cat

no, it is a skunk

do you like to jump rope

i think it is fun

when did you get that toy

can I play with it

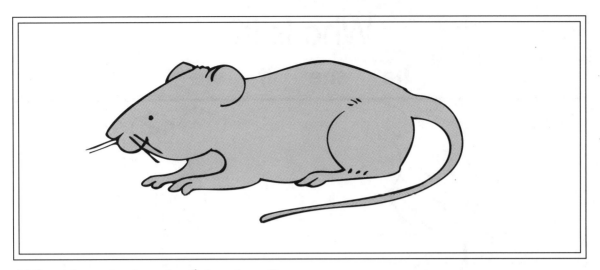

What is missing in this story?

Bud

C
<u>c</u>an you come over?

my pet rat bud got out

can you help me catch him

i got him

quick, get his pen

lock the lid

thank you

you were a big help

Who Is It?

he   she   it   we

Write.

he

Match.

it

we

she

he

Write.

He   She   We   it

Dad has a box.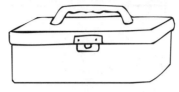

_____He_____ puts tools in _____it_____ .

Ted has a red kite.

_____ likes to fly _____ .

Ann and I got a big ball.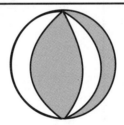

_____ play with _____ .

Betty has a bike.

_____ can ride _____ .

One and More Than One

Add <u>s</u> if it is more than one.

c u p		

The Toy Elephant

Color **one** orange.
Color **more than one** brown.

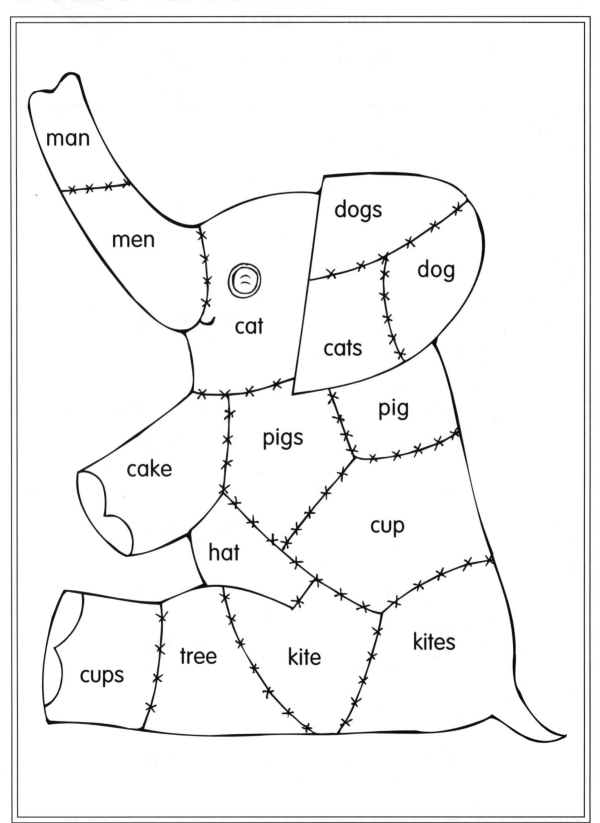

Making Smaller Words

is not - **isn't**

cannot - **can't**

do not - **don't**

Write.

1. That _isn't_ my cat.

2. I _____ find my kite.

3. I _____ want to go.

4. I _____ like snakes.

5. That _____ my dog.

6. Mom _____ go now.

Match.

isn't   cannot

don't   is not

can't   do not

Write.

1. Bob __cannot__ ride a bike.

    Bob __can't__ ride a bike.

2. I __do not__ want to go.

    I _____ want to go.

3. That __is not__ his pet.

    That _____ his pet.

4. We __cannot__ run in the street.

    We _____ run in the street.

Using <u>is</u> and <u>are</u>

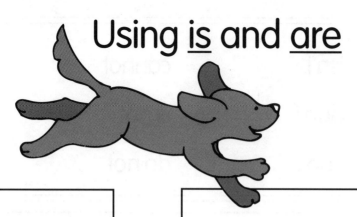

| one - **is** | more than one - **are** |

Circle the right word.

The dog (**is** **are**) small.

Sam and Tom (**is** **are**) here.

My kite (**is** **are**) yellow.

The cats (**is** **are**) playing.

We (**is** **are**) going to Disneyland.

What Does It Look Like?

Circle the picture that matches the words.

It is big.

It is tall.

It is black.

It is hot.

It is soft.

I see 3.

Find the Surprise

things you can do - Color **green.**
names of things -   Color **blue.**
how things look -   Color **red.**

box	nut	dog	pig
bed	big	red	ten	six	kite

pan	fast	tall	brown	fat	nest

| hop | | | | | sit |

| | yell | | | run | |

| | | skip | | | |

| fox | | | | sand | |

| TV | dig | tree |

Start at **a**.
Connect the dots.

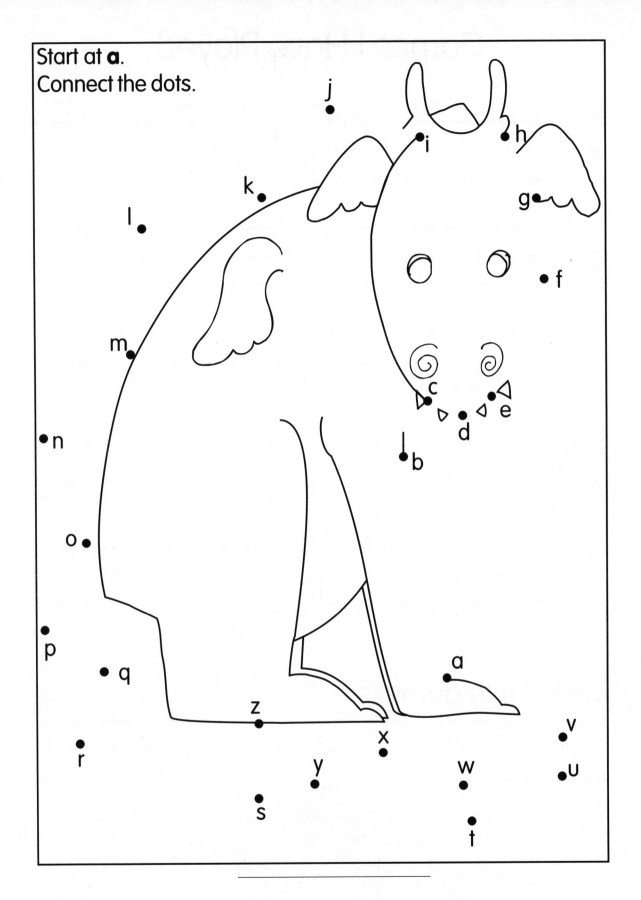

This dragon _____ green.

is   are

Games I Have Played

1. _____   6. _____

2. _____   7. _____

3. _____   8. _____

4. _____   9. _____

5. _____   10. _____

My favorite game is:

_____

_____

This is how to play _____ .

my favorite game

_____

- -

_____

- -

_____

_____

- -

_____

_____

- -

_____

- -

_____

Draw you and your friends playing the game.

When I was only one year old...

I couldn't...

_____

- -

_____

- -

_____

I was able to...

- -

_____

- -

_____

I looked like this.

When I am grown...

I will be able to...

_____

- -

_____

- -

_____

I won't be able to...

_____

- -

_____

- -

_____

I think I will look like this.

A New Pet

If I could have a new pet, I would get a:

_____

- -

_____

It would look like this:

I would name it:

_____

- -

_____

How to Make a Sandwich

1. Read   2. Cut   3. Paste in order

	1
	2
	3
	4
	5
	6

Cut the sandwich in two.

Open the jar
of peanut butter.

Eat it up!

Get out the bread,
peanut butter, and a knife.

Sit down and
take a big bite.

Put a lot of peanut butter
on the bread.

Do you like peanut butter and jelly sandwiches? _____

_____

What kind of sandwich do you like best?

_____

_____

_____

How do you make it?

_____

_____

_____

_____

_____

_____

_____

_____

How to Plant a Seed

1. Read   2. Cut   3. Paste in order

	1
	2
	3
	4
	5
	6

Water the seeds.

Pick out the seeds you want to plant.

Fill the hole with dirt and pat it down.

Now the seeds can grow.

Next you must dig a hole in the dirt.

Drop the seeds into the hole.

Draw what you think will grow from the seeds in the pot.

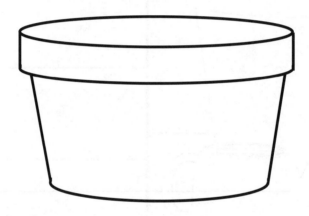

Skill: Arranges words in order to form a sentence.

hat was The red.

The hat was red.

Put the words in order to make a sentence.

1. funny.   That   was   pig   a

That was a funny pig.

2. you   Can   swim?

_____

3. pizza?   Do   like   you

_____

4. dog   down   ran   My   the   street.

_____

5. milk   Put   in   cup.   my   the

_____

Skill: Can write a statement and a question using correct end punctuation.

Write a telling sentence about this cat.

_____

_____

_____

Write an asking sentence about this cat.

_____

_____

_____

Skill: Identify proper nouns. A **proper noun** is the name of a <u>special</u> person, place, or thing.

Tom   Bishop School   Cheerios®

Put a ring around the proper nouns.

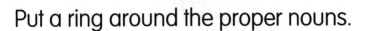

(Patty)   Jan   Barbie®

Goat   Yellowstone Park   Anna

What   Bob   Texas

Green Street   Jello®   Jose

Play   Ten   Tony

Skill: Begins proper nouns with a capital letter.

Amy   **J**amal   **K**elly

Write the names.

sam   Sam

tim

kisha

lee

mary

carlos

pete

joe

tina

rosa

Skill: Identifies words that tell what is happening. These **doing** words are
called **verbs**.

Put a ring around the doing words.

(run)   work   sing

red   trunk   cut

peek   swim   hat

Draw.

jump	sleep

Skill: Uses the correct forms of **doing** words (verbs) with added endings.

| jump | jumps | jump**ing** | jump**ed** |
| hop | hop**s** | hopp**ing** | hopp**ed** |

Put a ring around the right word.

The dog (run ⟨runs⟩) to get his dinner.

Bob and Tom (⟨run⟩ runs) to dinner too.

The kangaroo is (hopping   hopped).

He (hopping   hopped) all day.

The monkey (jumping   jumped) up in the tree.

It will (jump   jumps) to the top.

Connie (ride   rides) the bike.

Sam will (ride   rides) it next.

Matt is (looking   looked) for his pet.

He has (looking   looked) all day.

Skill: Recognizes and uses words that describe things. **Describing words** are called **adjectives**.

big   small

Match the picture and the words.
Put a line under the word that tells how it looks.

The box is big.
           ‾‾‾

It is sweet.

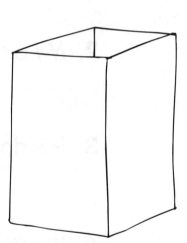

Get the black cat.

I saw six fish.

The oatmeal is hot.

My bunny is soft.

Skill: Identifies the two parts of a simple sentence. One part tells **who** or **what** the sentence is about. The other part tells **what happened**.

The monkey ate a banana.

The monkey - *who the sentence is about*
ate a banana - *what happened*

Put a ring around the **who** or **what** part.
Put a line under the **what happened** part.

1.  The girls went to the zoo.

2. My birthday cake fell on the floor.

3. His dogs barked all day.

4. The rain came down on my umbrella.

5. The children played a game.

6. The funny clown did tricks.

Skill: Recognize and use short vowel sounds in reading and spelling words.

a - pat   e - ten   i - in

o - hot   u - cup

Read and match.

fox

sun

pen

bat

six

6

Write.

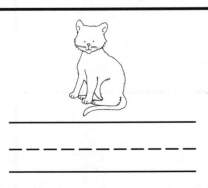

Skill: A word with a single vowel usually has the short sound.

cat **cup** **hop** **sit** **ten**

An **e** at the end of a one-syllable word usually makes the vowel long.

like **cake** **hope** **cute** **Pete**

Read.   Add an **e** and read again.

can	c a n e ⎯⎯	
cub	c u b ⎯⎯	
bit	b i t ⎯⎯	
tap	t a p ⎯⎯	
kit	k i t ⎯⎯	
rob	r o b ⎯⎯	

Skill: Recognize and use long vowel sounds in reading and spelling words.

a - cake   e - be   i - bike

o - go   u - cute

Read and match.

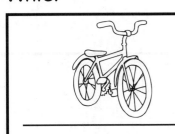

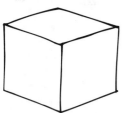

bee

kite

skate

cube

hose

Write.

_____

- - - - - - - - - - -

_____

_____

- - - - - - - - - - -

_____

_____

- - - - - - - - - - -

_____

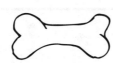

_____

- - - - - - - - - - -

_____

_____

- - - - - - - - - - -

_____

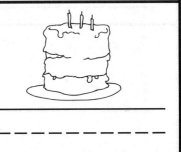

_____

- - - - - - - - - - -

_____

Skill: If two vowels are together in a one-syllable word, the first is usually long and the second is silent.

boat   sleep   tie   train

Read the words.
Match.

goat

paint

feet

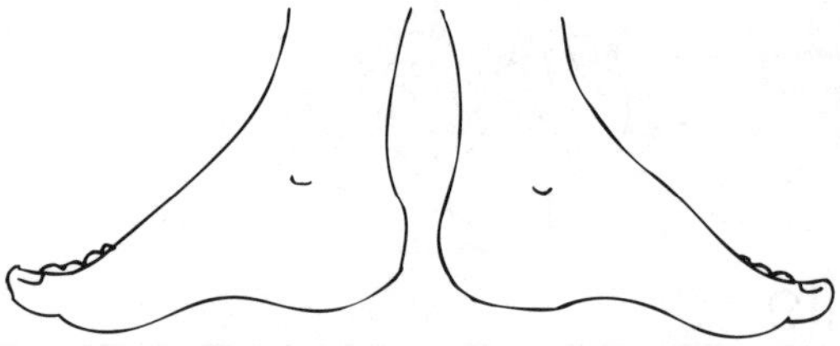

pie

Write.

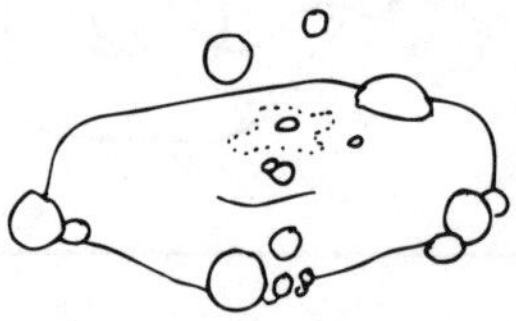

Skill: Reads and spells words containing vowels changed by an **r**.

An **r** following a vowel changes the vowel's sound.

ar - car	**er** - her	**ur**- fur
or - horn	**ir** - first	**wor** - worm

Read and fill in the missing letters.

H __er__ c _____

h _____ is beeping.

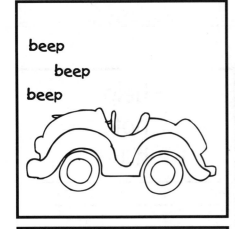

The cat's f _____

is _____ range.

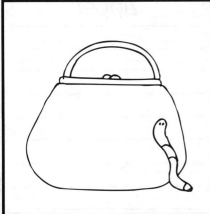

A fat _____ m

went up h _____

p _____ se.

Skill: Alphabetizes words using the second letter.

c**a**n	t**e**n	w**a**ll
c**e**nt	t**h**e	w**e**t
c**o**at	t**o**p	w**h**at

a b c d e f g h i j k l m n o p q r s t u v w x y z

Put these words in alphabetical order.

big	duck	help
bee	dad	hot
bag	did	hill

bag

run	tag	zoo
ring	trick	zebra
red	the	zipper

Answer Key

Please take time to go over the work your child has completed. Ask your child to explain what he/she has done. Praise both success and effort. If mistakes have been made, explain what the answer should have been and how to find it. Let your child know that mistakes are a part of learning. The time you spend with your child helps let him/her know you feel learning is important.

page 1

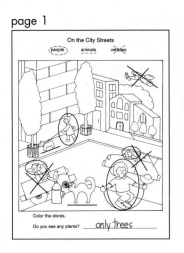

page 2

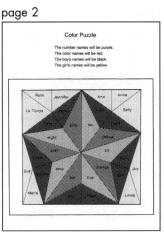

page 3

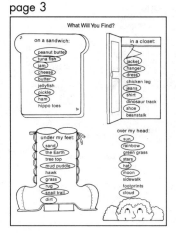

page 4

How many who words? 6
How many where words? 6
How many when words? 6

page 5

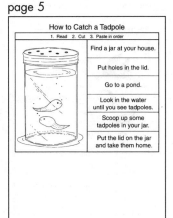

page 7

man	nut	hen
sun	bat	lid
bed	top	wig
cup	six	jet

page 8

1. yes
2. no
3. yes
4. yes
5. no
6. yes

page 9

1. yes 4. yes
2. yes 5. yes
3. no   6. no

page 10

drawings will vary

page 11

Write the words that rhyme in the boxes.

see	get	zoo
we	bet	moo
he	set	boo
bee	wet	too
three	let	shoe

boo	bee	three
bet	shoe	set
we	too	wet
let	he	moo

page 12

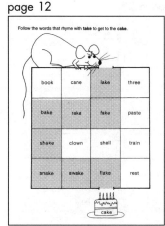

Follow the words that rhyme with **take** to get to the **cake**.

book	cane	lake	three
bake	rake	fake	paste
shake	clown	shell	train
snake	awake	flake	rest

page 13

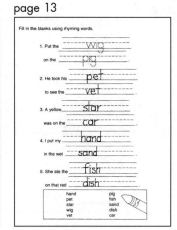

Fill in the blanks using rhyming words.

1. Put the ___ wig
   on the ___ pig
2. He took his ___ pet
   to see the ___ vet
3. A yellow ___ star
   was on the ___ car
4. I put my ___ hand
   in the wet ___ sand
5. She ate the ___ fish
   on that red ___ dish

hand	pig
pet	fish
star	sand
wig	dish
vet	car

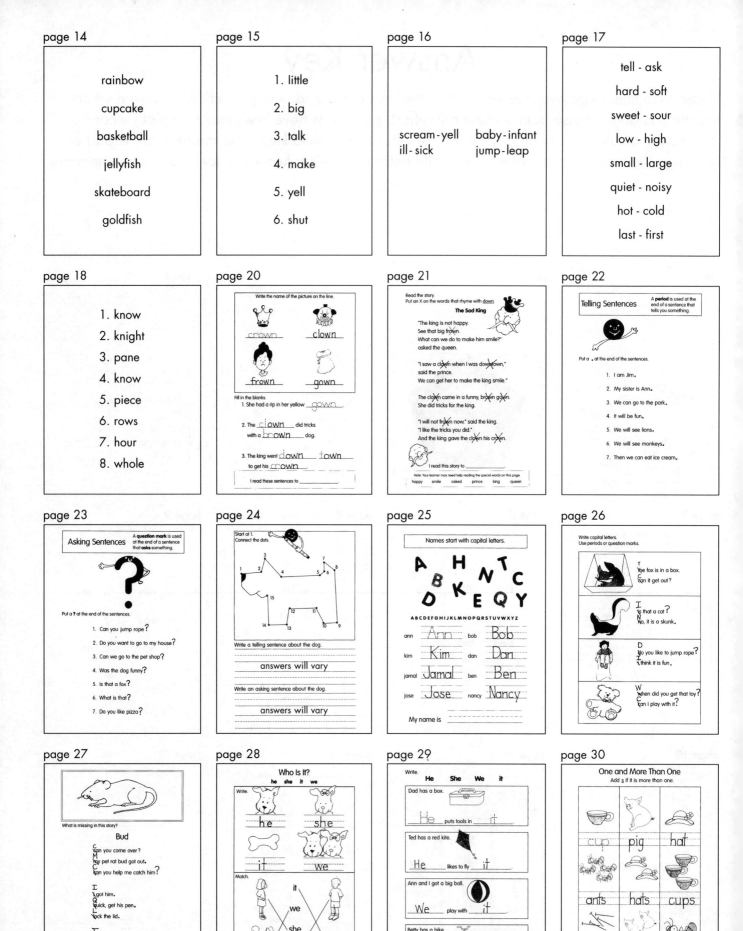

page 14

rainbow

cupcake

basketball

jellyfish

skateboard

goldfish

page 15

1. little
2. big
3. talk
4. make
5. yell
6. shut

page 16

scream - yell   baby - infant
ill - sick   jump - leap

page 17

tell - ask

hard - soft

sweet - sour

low - high

small - large

quiet - noisy

hot - cold

last - first

page 18

1. know
2. knight
3. pane
4. know
5. piece
6. rows
7. hour
8. whole

page 20

Write the name of the picture on the line.

crown   clown

frown   gown

Fill in the blanks.
1. She had a rip in her yellow gown.

2. The clown did tricks with a brown dog.

3. The king went down town to get his crown.

I read these sentences to _____

page 21

Read the story.
Put an X on the words that rhyme with down.

The Sad King

"The king is not happy.
See that big frown.
What can we do to make him smile?"
asked the queen.

"I saw a clown when I was downtown,"
said the prince.
We can get her to make the king smile."

The clown came in a funny, brown gown.
She did tricks for the king.

"I will not frown now," said the king.
"I like the tricks you did."
And the king gave the clown his crown.

I read this story to _____

Note: Your learner may need help reading the special words on this page.
happy   smile   asked   prince   king   queen

page 22

Telling Sentences   A **period** is used at the end of a sentence that tells you something.

Put a . at the end of the sentences.

1. I am Jim.
2. My sister is Ann.
3. We can go to the park.
4. It will be fun.
5. We will see lions.
6. We will see monkeys.
7. Then we can eat ice cream.

page 23

Asking Sentences   A **question mark** is used at the end of a sentence that **asks** something.

Put a ? at the end of the sentences.

1. Can you jump rope?
2. Do you want to go to my house?
3. Can we go to the pet shop?
4. Was the dog funny?
5. Is that a fox?
6. What is that?
7. Do you like pizza?

page 24

Start at 1.
Connect the dots.

Write a telling sentence about the dog.

answers will vary

Write an asking sentence about the dog.

answers will vary

page 25

Names start with capital letters.

A H N T C B K E Q Y D

ABCDEFGHIJKLMNOPQRSTUVWXYZ

ann   Ann   bob   Bob
kim   Kim   dan   Dan
jamal Jamal   ben   Ben
jose   Jose   nancy Nancy

My name is _____

page 26

Write capital letters.
Use periods or question marks.

The fox is in a box.
Can it get out?

Is that a cat?
No, it is a skunk.

Do you like to jump rope?
I think it is fun.

When did you get that toy?
Can I play with it?

page 27

What is missing in this story?

Bud

Can you come over?
My pet rat bud got out.
Can you help me catch him?

I got him.
Quick, get his pen.
Lock the lid.

Thank you.
You were a big help.

page 28

Who Is It?
he she it we

Write.

he   she

it   we

Match.

it
we
she
he

page 29

Write.
He   She   We   it

Dad has a box.
He puts tools in it.

Ted has a red kite.
He likes to fly it.

Ann and I got a big ball.
We play with it.

Betty has a bike.
She can ride it.

page 30

One and More Than One
Add s if it is more than one.

cup   pig   hat

ants   hats   cups

pins   pigs   ant

62 Answers

The Toy Elephant

Color **one** orange.
Color **more than one** brown.

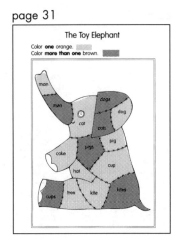

Making Smaller Words

is not - **isn't**
cannot - **can't**
do not - **don't**

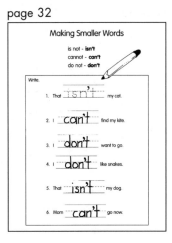

Write.

1. That __isn't__ my cat.
2. I __can't__ find my kite.
3. I __don't__ want to go.
4. I __don't__ like snakes.
5. That __isn't__ my dog.
6. Mom __can't__ go now.

Match.

isn't — cannot
don't — is not
can't — do not

Write.

1. Bob __cannot__ ride a bike.
   Bob __can't__ ride a bike.
2. I __do not__ want to go.
   I __don't__ want to go.
3. That __is not__ his pet.
   That __isn't__ his pet.
4. We __cannot__ run in the street.
   We __can't__ run in the street.

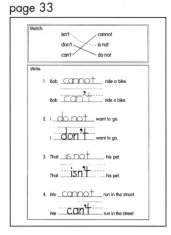

Using _is_ and _are_

one - **is**   more than one - **are**

Circle the right word.

The dog (**is** are) small.

Sam and Tom (is **are**) here.

My kite (**is** are) yellow.

The cats (is **are**) playing.

We (**is** are) going to Disneyland.

What Does It Look Like?

Circle the picture that matches the words.

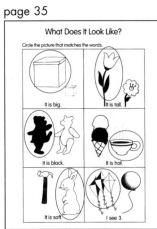

It is big. / It is tall. / It is black. / It is hot. / It is soft. / I see 3.

Find the Surprise

things you can do - Color **green**.
names of things - Color **blue**.
how things look - Color **red**.

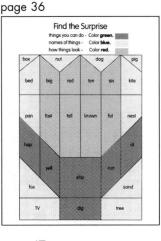

box / nut / dog / pig
bed / big / red / ten / six / kite
pan / fast / tall / brown / fat / nest
hop / sit
yell / run
skip
fox / sand
TV / dig / tree

Start at **a**.
Connect the dots.

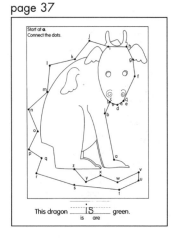

This dragon __is__ green.
         is   are

How to Make a Sandwich

1. Read   2. Cut   3. Paste in order

Get out the bread,
peanut butter, and a knife.

Open the jar
of peanut butter.

Put a lot of peanut butter
on the bread.

Cut the sandwich in two.

Sit down and
take a big bite.

Eat it up!

How to Plant a Seed

1. Read   2. Cut   3. Paste in order

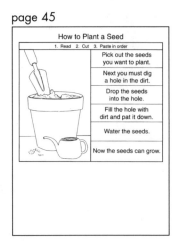

Pick out the seeds
you want to plant.

Next you must dig
a hole in the dirt.

Drop the seeds
into the hole.

Fill the hole with
dirt and pat it down.

Water the seeds.

Now the seeds can grow.

Skill: Arranges words in order to form a sentence.

hat was The red.
The hat was red.

Put the words in order to make a sentence.

1. funny. That was pig a
   __That was a funny pig.__
2. you Can swim?
   __Can you swim?__
3. pizza? Do like you
   __Do you like pizza?__
4. dog down ran My the street.
   __My dog ran down the street.__
5. milk Put in cup. my the
   __Put the milk in my cup.__
   Or — Put my milk in the cup.

Skill: Can write a statement and a question using correct end punctuation.

Write a telling sentence about this cat.

__answers will vary__

Write an asking sentence about this cat.

__answers will vary__

Skill: Identify proper nouns. A **proper noun** is the name of a **special** person, place, or thing.

Tom   Bishop School   Cheerios®

Put a ring around the proper nouns.

(Patty)   (Jan)   (Barbie®)
(Goat)   (Yellowstone Park)   (Anna)
What   (Bob)   (Texas)
(Green Street)   (Jello®)   (Jose)
Play   Ten   (Tony)

Skill: Begins proper nouns with a capital letter.

Amy   Jamal   Kelly

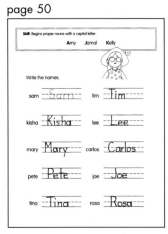

Write the names.

sam __Sam__   tim __Tim__
kisha __Kisha__   lee __Lee__
mary __Mary__   carlos __Carlos__
pete __Pete__   joe __Joe__
tina __Tina__   rosa __Rosa__

Skill: Identifies words that tell what is happening. These **doing** words are called **verbs**.

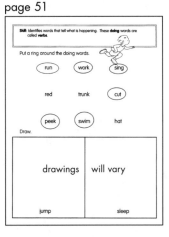

Put a ring around the doing words.

(run)   work   (sing)
red   trunk   (cut)
(peek)   (swim)   hat

Draw.

| drawings | will vary |

jump   sleep

Skill: Uses the correct forms of **doing** words (verbs) with added endings.

jump   jumps   jumping   jumped
hop   hops   hopping   hopped

Put a ring around the right word.

The dog (run (runs)) to get his dinner.
Bob and Tom ((run) runs) to dinner too.
The kangaroo is ((hopping) hopped).
He (hopping (hopped)) all day.
The monkey (jumping (jumped)) up in the tree.
It will ((jump) jumps) to the top.
Connie (ride (rides)) the bike.
Sam will ((ride) rides) it next.
Matt is ((looking) looked) for his pet.
He has (looking (looked)) all day.

Skill: Recognizes and uses words that describe things. **Describing words** are called **adjectives**.

big   small

Match the picture and the words.
Put a line under the word that tells how it looks.

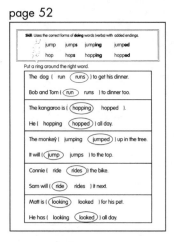

The box is big.
It is sweet.
Get the black cat.
I saw six fish.
The oatmeal is hot.
My bunny is soft.

page 54

Skill: Identifies the two parts of a simple sentence. One part tells **who** or **what** the sentence is about. The other part tells **what happened**.

The monkey ate a banana.
The monkey - *who the sentence is about*
ate a banana - *what happened*

Put a ring around the **who** or **what** part.
Put a line under the **what happened** part.

1. The girls went to the zoo.
2. My birthday cake fell on the floor.
3. His dogs barked all day.
4. The rain came down on my umbrella.
5. The children played a game.
6. The funny clown did tricks.

page 55

Skill: Recognize and use short vowel sounds in reading and spelling words.

a - pat   e - ten   i - in
o - hot   u - cup

Read and match.

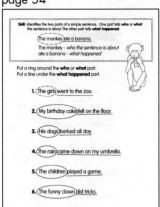

fox
sun
pen
bat
six

Write.

top	pig	pan
cat	bed	cup

page 56

Skill: A word with a single vowel usually has the short sound.

cat   cup   hop   sit   ten

An **e** at the end of a one-syllable word usually makes the vowel long.

like   cake   hope   cute   Pete

Read.   Add an **e** and read again.

can	c a n [e]	
cub	c u b e	
bit	b i t e	
tap	t a p e	
kit	k i t e	
rob	r o b e	

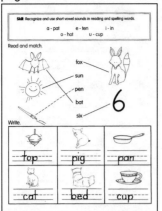

page 57

Skill: Recognize and use long vowel sounds in reading and spelling words.

a - cake   e - be   i - bike
o - go   u - cute

Read and match.

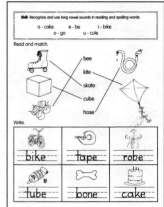

bee
kite
skate
cube
hose

Write.

bike	tape	robe
tube	bone	cake

page 58

Skill: If two vowels are together in a one-syllable word, the first is usually long and the second is silent.

boat   sleep   tie   train

Read the words.
Match.

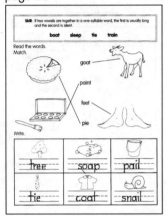

goat
paint
feet
pie

Write.

tree	soap	pail
tie	coat	snail

page 59

Skill: Reads and spells words containing vowels changed by an r.

An **r** following a vowel changes the vowel's sound.

ar - car   er - her   ur - fur
or - horn   ir - first   wor - worm

Read and fill in the missing letters.

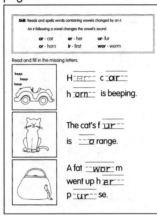

H er c ar
h orn is beeping.

The cat's f ur
is o range.

A fat wor m
went up h er
p ur se.

page 60

Skill: Alphabetizes words using the second letter.

can	ten	wall
cent	the	wet
coat	top	what

a b c d e f g h i j k l m n o p q r s t u v w x y z

Put these words in alphabetical order.

big	duck	help
bee	dad	hot
bag	did	hill
big	dad	help
bee	did	hill
big	duck	hot
run	tag	zoo
ring	trick	zebra
red	the	zipper
red	tag	zebra
ring	the	zipper
run	trick	zoo